MING'S ICEBERG

Kiri Lightfoot

Illustrated by
Kimberly Andrews

SCHOLASTIC
AUCKLAND SYDNEY NEW YORK LONDON TORONTO
MEXICO CITY NEW DELHI HONG KONG

For Sylvie, Lenny and Leia ~ K.L.

For Nova and Fern ~ K.A.

First published in 2021 by Scholastic New Zealand Limited
Private Bag 94407, Botany, Auckland 2163, New Zealand

Scholastic Australia Pty Limited
PO Box 579, Gosford, NSW 2250, Australia

ISBN 978-1-77543-713-0

A catalogue record for this book is available from the National Library of New Zealand.

12 11 10 9 8 7 6 5 4 3 2 1 1 2 3 4 5 6 7 8 9 / 2

Illustrated in Photoshop and Procreate

Publishing team: Lynette Evans, Penny Scown and Abby Haverkamp
Designer: Vida & Luke Kelly Design
Typeset in Catalina Clemente Bold
Printed in China by Toppan Leefung Printing Ltd

Scholastic New Zealand's policy is to use papers that are renewable and made efficiently from wood grown in responsibly managed forests, so as to minimise its environmental footprint.

Inside this egg is a brave explorer who starts her journey here, on the ice in Antarctica.

"This one is going to be an adventurer," said her parents.

They named her Ming, and as soon as she could waddle, they had to chase her everywhere she went.

One day, Ming was with her dad on an ice shelf looking at the horizon. "What's out there, where the sea meets the sky?" she asked.

"No penguin has been there," replied her dad.

"I might," said Ming.

She couldn't swim that far, and of course she couldn't fly, but every day Ming returned to the same spot.

"I wonder what's out there."

One day, Ming and her dad were sitting on the ice shelf when ...

GRUMBLE! CRACK!

The ice below them began to rumble and stir, rattle and shake.

A large crack appeared in the ice
and a massive chunk started to break away.

"ICEBERG! Run!" yelled her dad.

"Where is it going?" asked Ming.

"Out to sea!"

This gave Ming an idea. This was her chance.
"I'll be home soon!" she yelled, running towards the breaking ice.

She leapt over the huge crack and landed with a thud just as the iceberg broke away.

"Come back, Ming!"

But it was too late. Ming began to drift out to sea,
heading for the horizon at last.

Day became night, then night became morning.

Ming woke, hopeful that she had made progress,
yet the horizon didn't seem any closer.

There was something else that worried her too. The iceberg seemed to be getting smaller. "Or am I just growing?" she wondered.

Soon, she had a visitor.
"I wasn't expecting to see you here," said the giant bird.

"I'm an explorer, heading to where the sea meets the sky," said Ming.

"I'm an albatross. I've been flying these skies all my years, but I have never been there."

"Hi Albert Ross, I'm Ming. Don't worry, I will get there!"

"Well," said the bird,
"I hope it doesn't get too hot. Good luck!"

And off he flew.

Ming began to worry about what Albert Ross had said.
Maybe he was right. Maybe she wouldn't get to
where the sea meets the sky.
And what did he mean about it getting too hot?

CRACK!

A loud sound sang out across the seas.

WHOOSH!

Ming heard the sound of water, like a waterfall.

Days became nights and nights became new mornings ...
and all the while, Ming's iceberg melted.

It got smaller. It changed shape.

It began simply to disappear!

Just when Ming was beginning to lose hope, there was an enormous squirt of water in the air and a dark shadow under the sea.

A mighty whale
came to the surface.
"What are you doing
out here, little penguin?"

"I'm travelling to where the sea meets the sky," Ming replied. "But my iceberg is melting."

"I see," said the whale, whose name was Blue. "I've swum these seas for many years. I can tell you that the sea and the sky never meet."

"I shouldn't have come," whispered Ming, sadly.

"Ah, but wouldn't you have always wondered what was out here?" said Blue. "Now you know."

SCREEEECH!

"What's happening?" shouted Ming as her iceberg started to roll sidewards.

She started to slide down towards the sea. The iceberg was starting to flip...

"Jump!" yelled Blue.

So she did.

She jumped as high as she could into the air ...

and landed on Blue's back.

"It looks like it's time to go home," he said.
"Hold on ..."

So Ming and Blue began their journey home. As they travelled, a familiar shape appeared on the horizon. It was the most beautiful thing Ming had ever seen.

Antarctica. Home!

"Looks like your family are happy to see you," said Blue.

"Thanks for bringing me home," said Ming,
as she jumped back onto the ice.
"See you on the next adventure!"

And with a wave of a tail, Blue swam away.

Ming searched the crowd for her parents.

"You came home," said her dad. "It's so good to see you."

"I told you I would," said Ming.

"Did you find what you were looking for?" asked her mother.

"Well ... I found out how good it feels to come home!" said Ming.

"So, what's next?" asked her dad, knowing Ming would be looking for more adventures.

Something in the sky caught her eye. She was sure she could see Albert Ross flying in the distance.
"What's up there, where the mountains meet the sky?" she asked.

Ming's dad laughed. "Penguins can't fly, Ming!"

"I might," she smiled.

DID YOU KNOW?
• The continent of Antarctica is a huge, windy desert of ice. It holds the record for the lowest temperature ever recorded on Earth: minus 89.2°C.
• Emperor penguins are the largest of all penguins. They can't fly but are amazing swimmers and can hold their breath for over twenty minutes.
• Albatrosses have the largest wingspan of any bird, and make vast journeys at great speeds. They spend most of their life at sea.
• The Antarctic blue whale is the largest mammal ever to have lived on Earth – its tongue alone can weigh as much as an elephant!
ANTARCTICA